   Fight it 71
   Accept it 74

Chapter 9 – The Whole Process 77
   The end-to-end supply chain 77
   Work with it 78
   Take control 79

Chapter 9 – Efficiency Analysis 85
   Time cost calculations 85
   Process analysis 89
   Conclusion 95

Keyboard shortcuts 97
   (Near) Universal DAW keyboard shortcuts 97

Further reading 98

Ashley Hewitt – Efficient Music Production: How to Make Better Music, Faster

Published by Stereo Output Limited, company number 11174059

ISBN number 9781999600358

Copyright © Ashley Hewitt 2020

Ashley Hewitt has asserted his right under the Copyright, Designs and Patents Act 1988 to be identified as the author of this work.

All rights reserved. No part of this publication may be reproduced, stored in a retrieval system, or transmitted in any form or by any means, electronic, mechanical, photocopying, recording or otherwise, without the prior permission of the copyright holder except in the case of brief quotations embodied in critical views and certain other non-commercial uses permitted by copyright law.

Please go to www.stereooutput.com to contact us or follow us on various social media channels.

Stereo Output

Preface 1

Chapter 1 – Efficiency as a Concept 7
   What is efficiency? 7
   Why be efficient? 8
   Flow 9
   Output 11
   10,000 hours 12

Chapter 2 – Environment 17
   Your room 17
   Your setup 21

Chapter 3 – Your Knowledge 24
   RTFM 24
   Shortcuts 25
   Custom shortcuts 26
   Your time 32

Chapter 4 - Curation 35
   Sample curation 35
   Plugin curation 40
   Patch curation 41
   Template curation 41
   Melodic curation 44
   Make regular backups 45

Chapter 5 – Mixing & Arrangement 48
   Use send and return tracks 48
   Group and name tracks 49
   Add Markers 51
   Use a notepad 52
   Mix in order 54
   The final mix 57

Chapter 6 – Consider Individual Tasks 59

Chapter 7 – The Future 63
   Cloud Storage 63
   Cloud Mastering 66
   AI Composition 67

Chapter 8 – Staying Creative (And What To Do When You're Not) 71

Preface

At Highland Park, Michigan, in 1913, Henry Ford had a vision that would change the world forever.

Ford built cars. The Model T, introduced in 1908, was simple and relatively inexpensive. However, it was still costly, and cars were the preserve of the privileged few. Ford was determined to *"build cars for the great multitude"*. At the time, the average car took over 12 hours to build, and Ford understood that the key to reducing the cost of his cars was to build more of them, at a lesser cost.

Ford broke the Model T's assembly process down into 84 discrete steps, and converted his plant workers' roles from generalists to specialists in only a few of the 84 steps. He then hired an efficiency expert called Frederick Winslow Taylor to further analyse each step. One of Taylor's key methods was called the time and motion study, whereby he measured the average duration of each step, and then implemented measures to reduce that duration.

The cumulative effect of these small efficiencies was tremendous. It culminated in the streamlined process that became known as the assembly line, whereby the cars moved through each of the 84 steps on a belt moving at six feet per minute. The efficiency gains of the assembly line had quartered the average time it took to manufacture one car.

In 1924, Ford's 10 millionth Model T rolled off the assembly line, and thanks to its innovations and efficiency, Ford's dominance in the car market was sealed – for the time being at least. Their innovation had allowed Ford to cut prices in half and half again, from their starting price for a car of $850 in 1909 down to $290 by 1924.

In the early 1950s, Taiichi Onno also had a vision. Onno was an executive at Toyota's automotive division, having been brought over from Toyota's fabric manufacturing division to improve productivity and efficiency.

Toyota's philosophy at the time stemmed from a concept known as *Just-in-Time*. Toyota was not a particularly rich company and could not afford to waste money on excess equipment or materials – on that basis, everything was expected to be acquired not too early or not too late, using the minimum necessary resources. However, there were more efficiencies to be gained.

Onno experimented with many concepts in production between 1945 and 1955, and much of his work eventually became known as the Toyota Production System.

The four goals of the Toyota Production System were:

1) Provide world class quality and service to the customer.

2) Develop each employee's potential.

3) Reduce cost through the elimination of waste and maximise profit.

4) Develop flexible production standards based on market demand.

It is the third goal that we will focus on in this book – specifically the elimination of waste.

Onno identified seven types of waste:

1) Correction/scrap – this is where products are defective or require repairs.

2) Overproduction – this is where too many products are produced, or they are produced too early.

3) Waiting – this is where products are delayed for any reason.

4) Conveyance – this is the time products spend in transit between areas.

5) Processing – this is where more processing of a product takes place than what is necessary to achieve the desired result.

6) Inventory. This is where products and parts sit idle.

7) Motion. This is wasted movements, such as unnecessary turning, lifting and reaching.

The implementation of the Toyota Production System helped Toyota's automotive division expand rapidly. In 1957, the Toyota Crown became the first Japanese car to be exported to the United States. Toyota's growth has continued since, and Toyota is now the world's most dominant car manufacturer, with over 9% of the global market. The Toyota Production system still plays a key role within this dominance.

These two stories may seem lofty and irrelevant to you. You're a producer, in your studio, trying to make good music. You may even feel uncomfortable at the idea of applying manufacturing philosophy to such a pure artform, feeling manufacturing to be an alienating and dehumanising concept. However, it's simply a matter of scale. Car manufacturers may mass-produce products at billion-dollar budgets, but their challenges are the same as yours.

Your time is precious. You may be a professional musician fighting to compete against the thousands of tracks that enter the music market every single day, or you may be an amateur or semi-professional, delicately balancing your love of music production with the needs of your family and a day job. Either way, your time is your most limited resource, and using it correctly is the key to making a success of your work.

This book will contain a mix of ideas, from simple studio workflow tips to novel ways to think about your music production. Approach these with an open mind and open heart – the smallest gains translate to vast improvements over a long enough timeline.

I hope the methods in this book help you as much as they've helped me.

Chapter 1 – Efficiency as a Concept

What is efficiency?... Why be efficient?... Flow... Output... 10,000 hours...

What is efficiency?

Outside of writing music and writing about music, one of my main goals in my day job has been to help a company's processes become more efficient, by helping employees spend more time helping customers and less time on administration. During this, I've learned a great deal about what efficiency is, and how efficiencies are gained.

It is therefore worth us arriving at a common definition of what efficiency is and isn't.

Efficiency is not speed.

Although speed is one of the main byproducts of efficiency, being fast is not being efficient. Have you ever called a company and felt like they were trying to get you off the phone as quickly as possible? Maybe you had to call them multiple times to get your issue fixed? That is an example of a company whose management has confused speed with efficiency. Efficiency would have meant taking the time to solve your problem and looking at potential future problems so you didn't have to keep calling back.

Equally, spending three hours cooking a meal is not inefficient if you enjoy the process - even if the shop has a microwave meal you could have made in 10 minutes! What would be inefficient would be to go to the shop multiple times during the cooking process because you forgot to buy the right ingredients.

To conclude: efficiency is about **achieving maximum productivity with minimum wasted effort**.

Efficiency is catching a bus without spending twenty minutes stood at the bus stop.

Efficiency is answering your e-mails without wading through tons of junk.

Efficiency is spending every music production session working at your maximum creative potential.

Why be efficient?

It's a good question. Music production is fun, what does it matter if it's done inefficiently? Those of you with day jobs may produce music specifically as an escape from productivity targets, management, bureaucracy and corporate thinking. Why bring such a concept as efficiency into your safe musical space? The answers to these question lies in two worlds: psychology and mathematics.

Flow

Have you ever worked on a track and become so lost in the creative process that hours have passed without you even knowing? Have you ever created excellent music without consciously understanding how you did it? Have you ever reached for creative tools you didn't know you had? This is because of the flow state.

The flow state has been alluded to in philosophical texts for thousands of years, but was named by the psychologist Mihaly Csikszentmihalyi in 1975. Together with Jeanne Nakamura, they identified six attributes of flow (1):

1. Intense and focused concentration on the present moment
2. Merging of action and awareness
3. A loss of reflective self-consciousness
4. A sense of personal control or agency over the situation or activity

5. A distortion of temporal experience, one's subjective experience of time changes
6. Experience of the activity as intrinsically rewarding, also referred to as autotelic experience

Are these familiar to you?

Musicians often refer a great deal to the flow state. Have you ever heard a great producer say that when they produced a particular track, it felt like the music was coming through them, as if they were a lightning rod for some external creative force? This summarises the power of the flow state.

To quote Csikszentmiyalyi himself in an interview with *Wired* magazine, he described flow as *"being completely involved in an activity for its own sake. The ego falls away. Time flies. Every action, movement, and thought follows inevitably from the previous one, like playing jazz. Your whole being is involved, and you're using your skills to the utmost"*.

Flow is your highest state of creativity, it's your conscious mind stepping out of the way to let you accomplish a task. I find flow states to be one of the most rewarding, euphoric states in life.

Unfortunately, flow states aren't always easy to get into. There are distractions, from social media and news sites to computer crashes and thousands of useless samples on your hard drive. These distractions can disrupt the flow state, and if something disrupts your flow state, you cannot work to your highest potential. You can accomplish more in an afternoon of flow state than you can in a month of sloppy, distracted production – enabling this state through your environment and your actions is paramount to successful music production.

Output

Beyond the creative power of flow, you may have aspirations to carve out a career in music production or make it a lucrative hobby. There is no better way to enhance your profile in the music industry than to release music – and to release music regularly, you need to create music efficiently.

If you were to analyse your time spent writing music, you may find that you spend little of your time writing music, and spend a lot on the admin of writing music – finding samples, tweaking samples (in the same way each time), creating similar patches in different projects, creating mixdowns and then creating a different mixdown after making a change. It's important to minimise this administrative overhead to ensure that you maximise the time spent creating the core elements of your track, improvising and generating fantastic ideas – the elements of music creation that actually matter.

10,000 hours

You may have heard of the 10,000 hours concept, ever since it was popularised by Malcolm Gladwell's book *Outliers*.

In 1993, Anders Ericsson, a Professor at the University of Colorado, wrote a paper called *The Role of Deliberate Practice in the Acquisition of Expert Performance*. The paper discussed the work of a group of psychologists who had studied the practice habits of violin students from childhood to adulthood.

All had begun playing at a primary school age with similar practice times. However, at age eight, differences between practice times had begun to emerge. By age 20, the best performers had averaged more than 10,000 hours each, while the weaker performers had amassed as little as 4,000 hours each. The difference between the best violinists and merely good violinists was as little as 2,200 hours in accumulated practice:

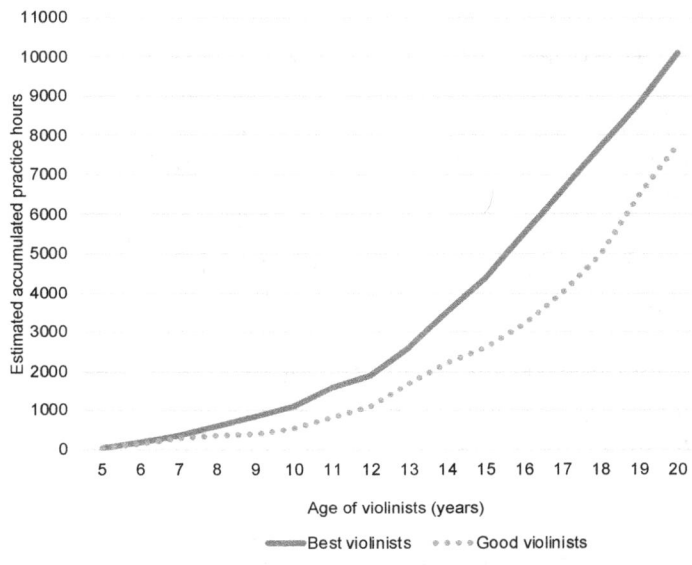

Reproduced from The Role of Deliberate Practice in the Acquisition of Expert Performance, Ericsson et al, 1993

Key to this study was that the psychologists speculated that talent would play a role, and big differences, attributable to natural talent, would begin to emerge between the violinists around 5,000 hours – but these differences didn't emerge. The main differentiating factor between the violinists age 20 was simply time spent practicing.

Ericsson concluded that *"many characteristics once believed to reflect innate talent are actually the result of intense practice extended for a minimum of 10 years"*.

Now I appreciate that 10,000 hours is an arbitrary figure – there's no question that it's famous due to its memorability rather than being an exact figure. Furthermore, the semantic definition of expertise is subjective. Despite this, the fact is this – the more time you spend doing something, the more your mastery of it you will acquire.

Let's use 10,000 hours as our goal and analyse how long it would take to reach this goal based on 30 hours per week of music production:

Goal:	10000 hours
Practice per week:	30 hours
Time required:	6 years 4 months

This seems reasonable. But this assumes that you spend 100% of your time producing music actually producing music.
However, if you're an inefficient producer, your time spent on production may look something like this:

Social media:	20%
News sites etc:	5%
Watching tutorials:	5%
Process inefficiencies:	30%
Music production:	40%

This means that only 40% of the 30 hours allotted to making music is spent actually making music. This means the 10,000 hour goal would look like this:

Goal:	10000 hours
Efficiency:	40%
Practice per week:	30 hours
Time required:	15 years 11 months

You'll never be 100% efficient, and that's fine. But if you can double your efficiency, it'll halve the time required to reach 10,000 hours, down to a reasonable 8 years:

Goal:	10000 hours
Efficiency:	80%
Practice per week:	30 hours
Time required:	7 years 11 months

As I've previously mentioned, the 10,000 hours figure is arbitrary. What I'm trying to highlight, however, is that small efficiency gains in the short term translate to massive gains in the long term – and this is a theme I'll delve further into towards the end of this book. Even if you only implement one tip from this book, the effect will be transformative enough on your work that you will gain huge amounts of time over the lifetime of your music production career. Let's get stuck in!

Chapter 2 – Environment

Your room… Your setup…

Your room

It sounds perverse that your environment would contribute so strongly to the efficiency of your music production processes, however it is fundamental. You will not reach your potential as a musician in the wrong environment.

The first element to consider is whether your environment facilitates the easy production of music. Jamming on your laptop with headphones on while your family watches TV is fine to a certain extent, but if you're serious about making music you need an environment dedicated to music production.

To do this, I suggest starting with your monitors. They exist to reproduce the sound you create, and inaccuracies in the reproduction of your sound will make you overcompensate for these inaccuracies, and you will have to redo your mixes again and again when these mixing mistakes reveal themselves on superior sound systems.

You therefore need to invest in a good quality pair of studio monitors (the Yamaha HS series tend to be well-reviewed for those of you on a budget), and place these correctly.

Monitor placement is an extraordinarily complex subject (and worthy of a book in of itself) but at a minimum they should be 2 feet away from the walls of your room and angled at towards your ears at an equal distance from your primary mixing position, creating a triangle, ideally an equilateral one:

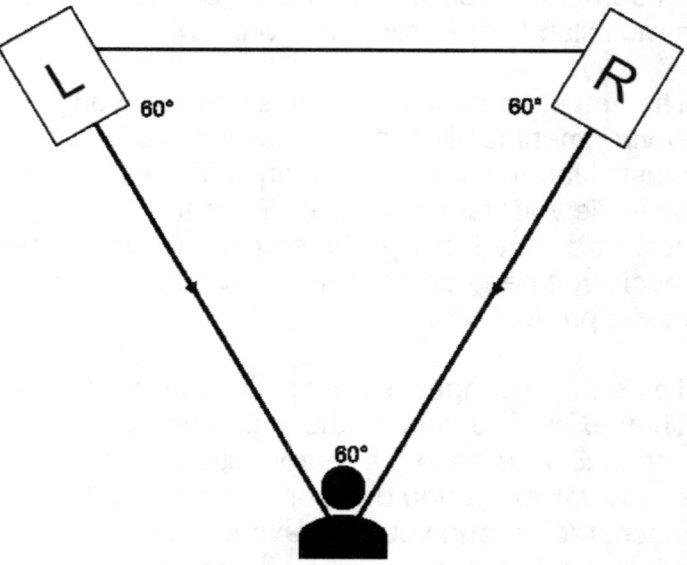

Even with your monitors placed correctly, your room's dimensions will mathematically emphasise and de-emphasise certain bass frequencies due to standing waves.

Every sound wave frequency has a wavelength. When wavelengths are mathematical partials to the size of your room, standing waves are generated. For example, a 60Hz sound wave has a wavelength of 5.72 meters. If your room is 5.72 meters, the peaks and troughs of a 60Hz sound wave within it will always stay in the same parts of your room as they reflect off the walls. The same effect will be found at frequencies octaves above the fundamentals, i.e. at 120Hz, 240Hz, etc.:

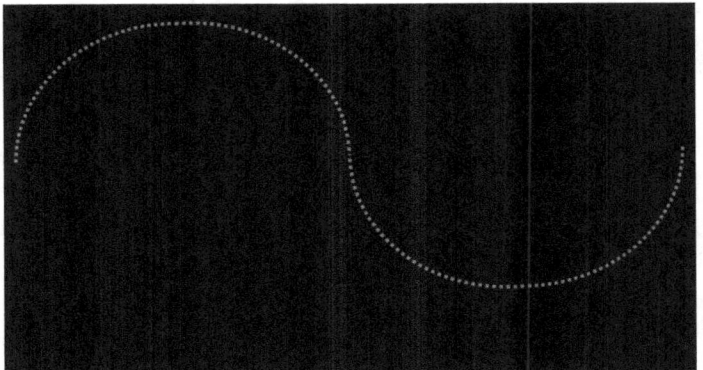

A 60Hz sound wave in a 5.72m room

You can experience these waves for yourself – simply measure your room and, using an online calculator, calculate the frequency that will correspond to two wavelengths. Play a sine wave corresponding to that frequency, and walk around your room – you will hear areas where the waveforms cancel each other out, and you will hear areas where the waveforms compound each other. Now, just imagine you have a static listening position somewhere within this – you will either hear far more bass than is in your track, or far less – either way, it's not accurate!

Where possible, you should use a room that corresponds to what's known as golden mean calculations – this is where no surface dimensions (length, width and height) are multiples of each other. For example, a room with a 2m ceiling shouldn't have a width or length of 4m, 6m, 8m, etc.

Failing that, you need to treat your room. Not only are standing waves an issue, but your room's walls will reflect some higher frequencies back towards you, and so it is worth investing in bass traps and acoustic absorbers to maximise the accuracy of your sound reproduction. You may wish to, if you have a good budget, finding bass traps that are tuned to the dimensions of your room.

If you're on a tight budget, you can still invest in good studio treatment – you can create a passable DIY bass trap with timber, fabric and insulation, as long as you're willing to spend a sunny afternoon constructing it.

I recommend *Sound On Sound's* article *Studio SOS Guide To Monitoring & Acoustic Treatment* for a solid introduction to the topic of room treatment.

Your setup

Beyond your monitors, there are additional factors to consider. Is your chair comfortable? Are your computer or mixer controls all within easy reach? Are your most-used tools nearest to you? Is your room clean and free of mental distractions?

Most professional studios place the mixing desk in the centre, the effects units under the mixing desk and less-used tools away from the centre.

This allows the producer to stay in the optimal position for mixing the vast majority of the time. As an example, look at this mastering studio's setup:

Notice how the effects units are all within easy reach of the centre, with the monitors forming a triangle with the centre point. In this studio, the computer is not the primary tool, so it is placed to one side.

If this was a studio based around the computer, they would place the computer in the centre of the studio, allowing the engineer to remain in the optimal listening position while performing the required tweaks.

If you produce using a computer, aim for screen space – either by using multiple computer monitors or using a high resolution screen like an iMac. Switching between screens is a waste of time.

The internet, and social media in particular, is a tremendous distraction. Nothing can disrupt your flow quicker than reading something on the news or watching some video or other on social media. Unless it's required, I'd recommend disconnecting your studio computer from the internet – even when taking breaks, your creative mindset is delicate, and any stimulation outside of it can shatter your flow.

Look for other distractions in your room. Do you have clutter? Irrelevant artwork? Sources of interruption? You should optimise every element to minimise distraction and enhance your flow.

One further source of distraction and irritation can be the computer itself. Is it fast enough to handle audio processing? Does it ever crash? Do you have to spend time muting, soloing and freezing tracks to play back your music? If so, it may be worth investing in an upgrade.

Chapter 3 – Your Knowledge

RTFM… Shortcuts… Custom shortcuts… Your time…

RTFM

You're likely aware of the initialism RTFM – it stands for *Read The F*cking Manual*. I know that as producers, many of us don't enjoy doing this. We know how to use software, right? We know how to play an instrument, right? However, it's paramount to read the manual of any new software you acquire.

I am an Ableton Live user, and I recently needed to export the stems of an EP for a label. To do this, I soloed each track and bounced it. This process took an hour for one song.

Only by Googling did I discover that there was a function specifically designed to do this (select *All Individual Tracks* when exporting). You're probably screaming at these words right now – how could I use Ableton for over five years and never know about this function? It's easy. I didn't RTFM.

I'm in no doubt that if you haven't RTFM for the software you use, you're likely wasting your own time in exactly the same way I wasted mine, without even knowing it. Software engineers love efficiency, and modern software updates are often designed to automate repetitive tasks. This means it's always worth taking the time to read the manual of your software, and the release notes of any updates – it could save you hours or even days in the long run.

Shortcuts

One of the most important element of RTFM is keyboard shortcuts. The power of knowing all shortcuts is transformative - it can take your workflow from dragging a mouse laboriously to fully flowing with your DAW. It's necessary, unfortunately, to learn shortcuts by practice and repetition, but you will work at unparalleled efficiency and speed once they're embedded within your memory.

Beyond learning keyboard shortcuts, you can embed these into your workflow by buying a computer keyboard cover with the shortcuts for your DAW overlaid on the keys. You could also buy a gaming mouse such as this one:

And map your most common shortcuts to the extra buttons.

Besides mapping shortcuts permanently, I would suggest mapping your MIDI controller to a particular parameter you're working heavily on - not only will it feel more intuitive but recording automation will give you more honest results than entering the automation with a mouse.

I've added a section that sets out the most common keyboard shortcuts at the back of this book.

Custom shortcuts

You can also create custom keyboard shortcuts in a growing number of DAW packages – I'll show you the process in Ableton Live and Logic Pro X.

Ableton Live doesn't (as of writing) allow for custom keyboard shortcuts in the traditional sense – you can't, for example, map a traditional Ctrl + key shortcut. To some extent this makes sense; Ableton's design is feature-rich without forcing you to work through menus.

Despite this, there may be regular features you use during a production section – and for this reason, there is an Ableton function called *Key Mappings*.

While in Ableton, simply press Ctrl + K (or ⌘ + K on Mac) and ensure your Browser is visible. Then, press a function on your screen using your mouse, then press a key to map it to that key. For example, I can map the metronome to the I key and phase the track up and down with the 1 and 2 keys:

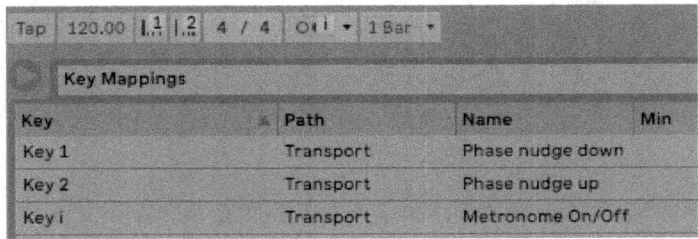

However, it gets better than this! For dynamic effects (rather than on/off), you can map a minimum and maximum value to a keypress, as I have done with this Delay:

| Key 3 | 2-MIDI | Delay | Dry/Wet | 0.0 % | 55 % |

This means that pressing the 3 key will cycle this Delay to 0 or 55% Wet.

This is particularly useful for regular functions, including moving your master fader between 0dB and -6dB to check your mix, or cycling your output between Mono and Stereo to check your track's mono compatibility.

Do note, however, that only keys that do not have a function or existing shortcut within Ableton Live will work as key maps. As of writing, the following keys are available for key mapping:

Key mappings only work in that particular Ableton file, so if you find yourself using particular mappings on a regular basis, I suggest you create a new Ableton file (with any other configurations you usually use), and save it as the default new set from the *File | Folder* section of the Preferences menu:

Preferences

Look			
Feel	Save Current Set as Default	Save	Clear
	Create Analysis Files	On	

Whereas custom shortcuts are only available in single Ableton projects, Logic Pro X (as well as other DAWs, including Studio One) allow you to create your own central keyboard shortcuts, that stay with you regardless of which project file you're in.

To create custom keyboard shortcuts in Logic, click on Logic Pro X in the top-left corner, then hover over Key Commands and click on Edit to open the Key Commands menu.

Rather than Ableton's click-and-tap approach, Logic's approach involves a menu, which contains every global Logic command:

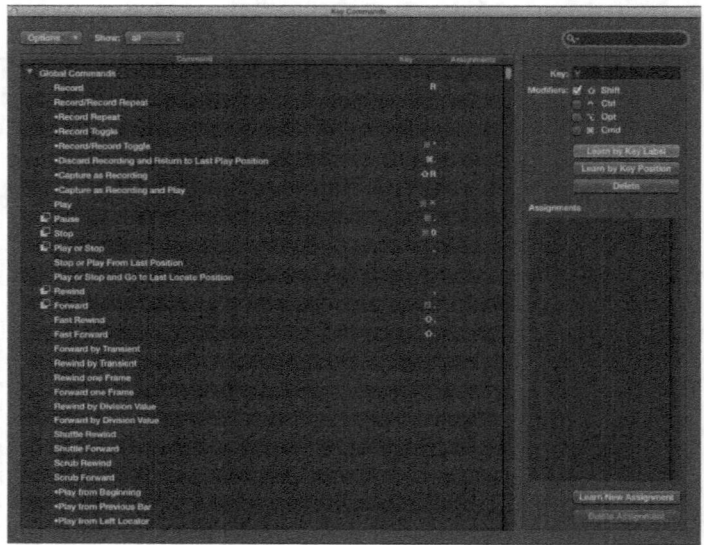

To assign a new key command, use the search bar in the top-right and find the function you want. Then, click on Learn by Key Label, click on the function you want to assign that shortcut to, and then press the shortcut you wish to create on your keyboard. In this instance, I have assigned Create New Instrument to Shift + Y:

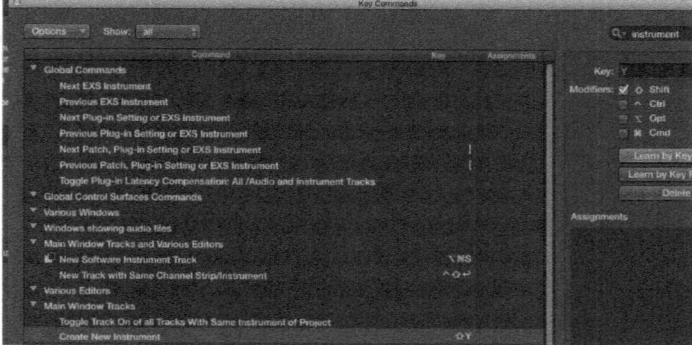

When doing this yourself, you may find that there are so many keyboard shortcuts in place in Logic that you have difficulty finding key assignments. I suggest you study existing keyboard shortcuts first, to find spare combinations to use, or find existing shortcuts mapped to easy-to-remember key commands that you're rarely going to use – that way, you can overwrite them.

You can also use the *Learn New Assignment* function – simply click on *Learn New Assignment* and use a control function on your MIDI controller to assign Logic commands to your MIDI controller.

If you use Logic on multiple systems, you can export your keyboard shortcuts for import to your other systems – that way, they're always available to you.

As you can see, there's a huge amount of customization available in both Ableton and Logic. Other DAWs also have this level of customization available – I've only highlighted Logic and Ableton due to their differing methods.

Over time, learning shortcuts are a significant improver to both your efficiency and your experience of making music with a DAW, bringing it far closer to the feeling of jamming and away from the feeling of programming a computer.

Your time

Time management is paramount, and being aggressive about defending your own time will pay off hugely in the long term. Time is your only non-renewable resource, and you should ideally book it out within a calendar or calendar app. This means you can design your life around your music production, not vice versa.

However, that's not to say that you'll always be producing music. Everyone needs their downtime, and everyone inevitably has time when they're not able to produce (for example, due to a long journey with family). This downtime can still be used - there is an abundance of resources for learning about music production, from books (such as this one) to video tutorials.

The problem with these, especially with video tutorials, is that applying your knowledge during a production session can disrupt your flow, displacing your original ideas with whatever you've just read. It's helpful to acquire new techniques, but do this in your downtime, letting ideas percolate before applying them during your studio time.

Another way to harness your idle time is to realise that there's actually an abundance of fantastic software coming to the market now that allows you to sketch out ideas on your mobile phone or tablet.

For example, the superb Caustic by Single Cell Software that is very reminiscent of early versions of Propellerhead Reason:

Alternatively, Korg has several mobile apps that simulate their hardware synthesizers – you could even plug your phone into your DAW and use it as an external instrument should you wish to include your ideas in a track:

Chapter 4 - Curation

Sample curation... Plugin curation... Patch curation... Template creation… Make regular backups…

Sample curation

If your music uses samples, sample curation is one of the most important elements of production. When you dig into your samples, you should feel like a TV chef opening a pantry full of the highest quality, freshest, most colourful goods - not like someone on *Storage Hunters*, wading through piles of rubbish hoping to find something of value.

Samples 4.75 GB

Add Tags...

▼ General:
Kind: Folder
Size: 4,745,508,612 bytes (4.78 GB on disk) for 11,973 items

This is a relatively small sample folder. In spite of this, it feels unlikely that all 12,000 samples are valuable.

A huge amount of your time is wasted by samples - by auditioning poor-quality samples you will never use, and by spending too much time tweaking a weak sample to make it more suitable for your production.

It's always worth investing in good quality samples, as a perfectly tweaked poor sample will never match the quality of a great, un-tweaked sample.

Once you've acquired your samples, it's worth labelling them and then saving them in an organised folder (e.g. kicks or vocals). With your samples organised, analyse them once every few months – which are your most-used samples? Which are the samples you thought you'd use, but you didn't? Which are no use to you? Clear out the ones you don't use or aren't any use.

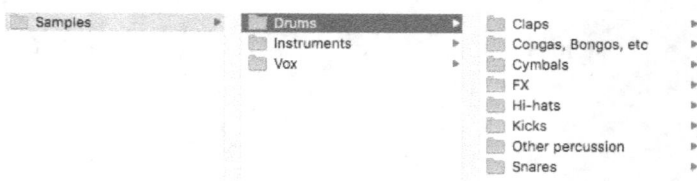

If you have tweaked a sample, it takes a matter of seconds to bounce that sample into your sample folder - do so when it's possible you'll use the sample in the future. The worst-case scenario is that you have a well tweaked sample you do not use and clear out in a few months' time.

Beyond that, you can bounce useful loops from otherwise poor tracks for future projects. For example, in Logic Pro X, you can right-click on a clip, go to Export and click on Add to Loop Library to add your loop to your Apple Loops library for future use.

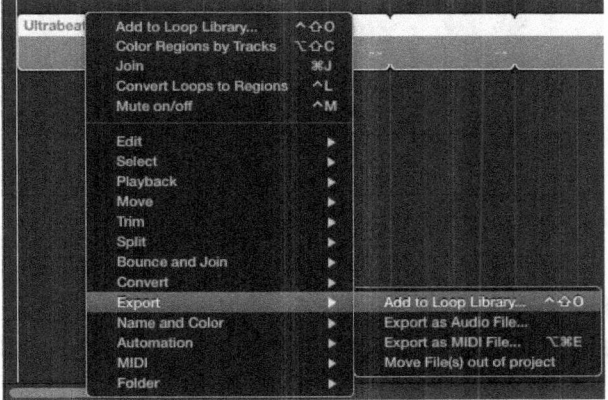

Equally, in Ableton, you can export MIDI loops quickly through the Export Audio/Video dialog. Just remember to Normalize the track if it's particularly quiet and select Create Analysis File for easy preview and use:

If you have multiple samples (or copies of samples) grouped together on a single track in Ableton, you can also retain this loop for future use. Simply right-click on the group of samples and click on Consolidate:

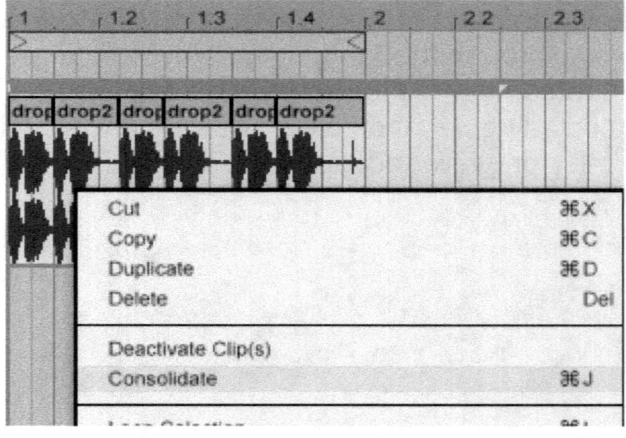

Then, click on your consolidated sample and go into the Clip view:

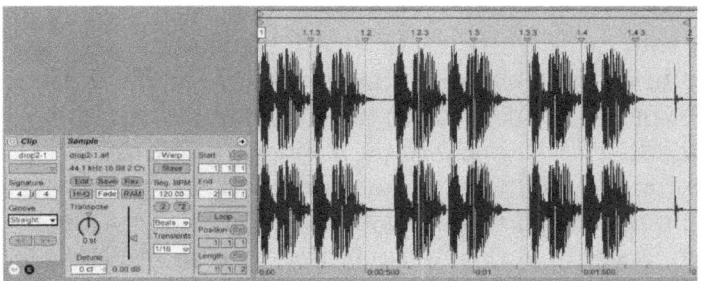

Once you're in Clip View, right-click on the sample name and click on Show In Browser:

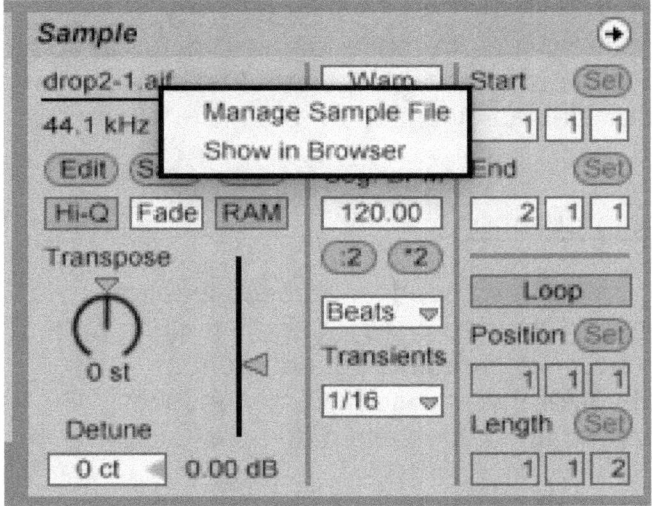

This will display your new, consolidated sample in Ableton's browser:

From here, you can simply right-click on the file name and click on Show In Finder (or Show In Explorer on Windows) and it will show you the location of the file within a Finder/Explorer window. From here, you can copy and paste the sample to your own sample/loops folder – just make sure you rename it *after* you've moved it.

This may seem slightly arduous upon first reading, but it's worth it – it only takes ten seconds when you're used to the process, and you can build up your own loop library of completely custom-made loops – unique to you, with no worries about copyright (assuming your source files are licensed for use!).

Plugin curation

Plugins are a wonderful source of inspiration, especially the free ones – there's nothing better than hearing incredible sounds from a synthesizer that only took 60 seconds to download and install and didn't cost a penny.

However, not all plugins are as suited to your production style as they initially seem, and they can clutter up your workflow and be a source of system instability when overused.

You should clear out plugins you don't immediately take a shining to – it's very rarely the case you will need them. Doing this also enhances your knowledge, as focusing on deriving the best sound from one synthesizer will teach you more about synthesis than flitting between different synthesizers hoping to stumble across the right sound. You should be able to articulate a role and reason for every single plugin you own, and love the plugin for its functionality. If it doesn't meet this test, it is disposable.

Patch curation

Plugins often arrive with a huge number of patches, but it's your own patches that are most important. You can treat these just like samples – if you make a patch you like, save it. If you tweak a preset to your satisfaction, save it.

I also suggest that you save a copy of your custom patches to your samples folder – that way, should you store your samples in the cloud (we'll discuss that later), you can easily retrieve your VST patches in addition.

Template curation

Remember that you can save any repetitive action, and you can compile these into templates. Do you have a normal setup for production in your DAW, for example two drum machines, a bass and a lead? If so, load up the right plugins and effects unit and save it. In Logic Pro X, you can do this by saving your project as a template:

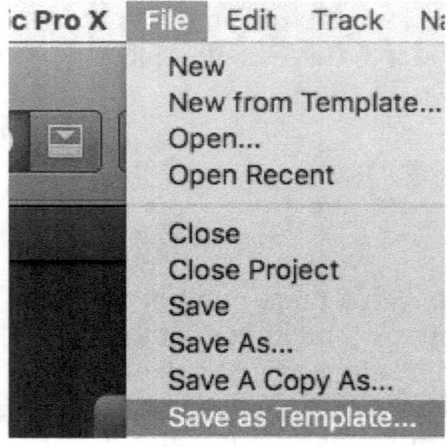

Equally, in Ableton, you can save any .als file into the Templates section of your Library for easy retrieval:

Do you have a mainstay synthesizer you use for particular sounds? If so, create some basic starting patches. If you always use a fat supersaw sound in your tracks, create a fat unprocessed supersaw patch and save it. Do you always start with the same drum kit? If so, tweak it according to how you would normally tweak it and save it.

Beyond that, you can save your parameters as the default setting in both Logic Pro X:

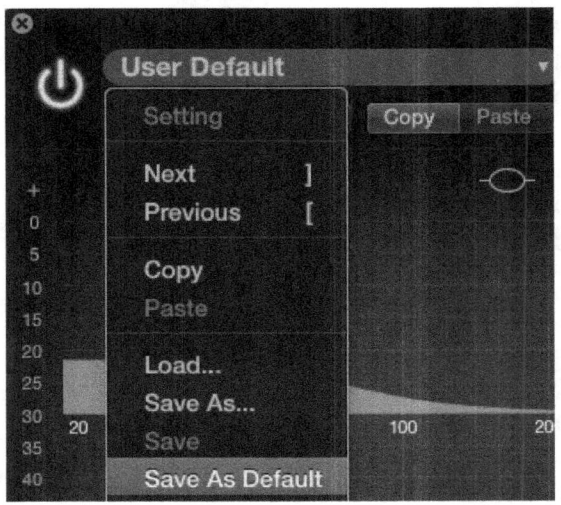

And in Ableton Live:

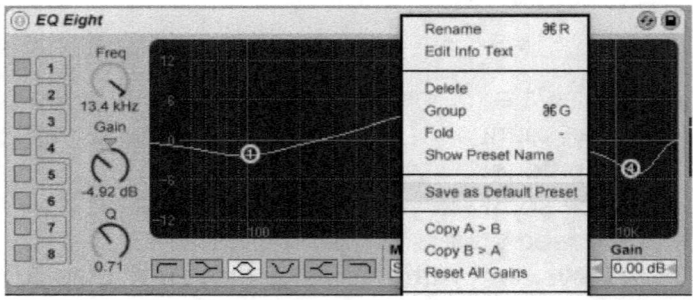

Melodic curation

Beyond saving samples and patches, it's worth realising that even though many of your jam sessions won't produce a finished track, or even a developable idea, it doesn't matter. The constituent parts of your jam sessions can often contain something useful. Many a track I've made has been composed of recycled parts from smaller jam sessions. Some of the wackier sounds you composed can even be used as subtle background sound effects.

A useful timesaver can be to label your saved DAW sessions with a tempo and key, so that if you're ever working on a track in a similar key and looking for parts, you know where to look. Then, in Logic for example, you can go to File -> Import and choose which elements of another project you wish to import into your existing project:

Num.	Name	Content	Plug-ins	Sends
1	Stabs		Sylenth...	
2	stab it		Sylenth...	
3	Audio 4		Compre...	
4	Glide		Sylenth...	
5	Delayed rim		Ultrabe...	
6	Noise hit		ES2, Ch...	
7	Hovering glass lead		Sculptu...	
8	Quiet laser		Retro S...	
9	Background noise		Compre...	
10	Vox		Compre...	

I suggest importing everything you may find useful – it's far quicker to audition and delete anything unhelpful than to import and audition each track one at a time.

Make regular backups

I hope, just like contents insurance, you never need to use a backup. However, disaster can strike at any time – this can range from a corrupted DAW session to a hard drive that does nothing but click when you try to boot your computer. It's not pretty.

Recovering from a data loss is one of the most inefficient things you can do in music production – and that assumes that it is a recoverable data loss. Backups are what's required to mitigate against this risk.

Whilst I cannot guarantee that you'll never lose your data, there are simple, efficient practices that can help you.

At a minimum, you should follow the 3-2-1 backup rule, which states:

3) Keep at least three copies of your data – the copy that you're working on and two copies of that.

2) Store two backup copies on different devices or storage media. All storage media fails over a long enough timeline, and two of the same storage media are likely to fail at similar times. On this basis, consider using your primary HDD, an external flash media drive and a copy in the cloud.

1) Store at least one backup copy offsite. This means you always keep one backup copy outside your house – whether this be a hard drive at a trusted friend or relative's house or, even better, in the cloud.

I follow this system – I have my main HDD, an external USB drive plugged in which takes automatic Time Machine backups on a daily basis and I regularly manually upload my data to the cloud. It's by no means a foolproof, guaranteed method of keeping my files forever, but it's a good enough compromise between time and redundancy that's kept me out of a fair few scrapes over the years – and it's certainly better than nothing!

To summarise this chapter: samples, plugins, patches, templates (and backups of all these) are the building blocks of your music and your processes, and if you have these in order, your music production will be swift and effective.

Chapter 5 – Mixing & Arrangement

Use send and return tracks... Group and name tracks... Add markers... Use a notepad... Mix in order... The final mix

Use send and return tracks

When composing and mixing, you sometimes want precision. However, in the early stages of the mix, you're often curious about how a particular effect would sound added to your track. Adding an individual effect can be arduous, and it's more efficient to harness the technique that producers in the analogue days had to use due to cost limitations of hardware: send and return tracks.

Not only is this a CPU-efficient way of producing music, but it makes your decision-making faster. For example, you could map four different return tracks with different effects:

| A Reverb | B Delay | C Saturator | D Chorus |

With these mapped, you can then send your individual channels to any extent you want. In this example, the use of send and return channels has saved the time it would have taken to set up seven different effects units:

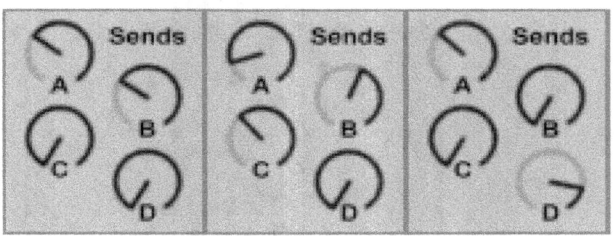

Group and name tracks

Send and return channels are not the only way to speed up your workflow. To name and categorise your individual tracks is correct, but I=it's so easy not to do it. Creative flow can lead you to ignore the task until you find yourself utterly lost in your arrangement, having to solo individual tracks to establish what they are.

I recommend three levels of categorisation:

1. Naming tracks according to a convention, e.g. Kick 1, kick layer high-pass, main hi-hat, secondary hi-hat:

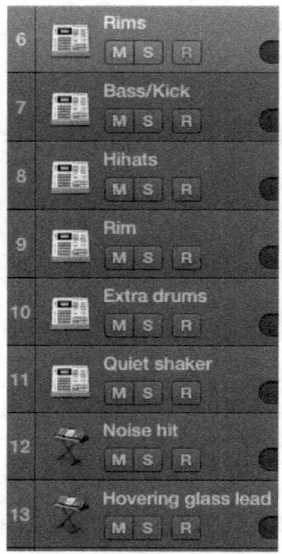

2. Grouping tracks by type, e.g. Drums, vox, synths, etc:

3. Colouring & naming individual MIDI clips:

Drums intro	Drums main drop		
	Hi-hats	Additional hi-hats	
		Fill	Fill

Add Markers

Another way to keep yourself grounded in your work is to use markers in your sequence to delineate the corresponding areas.

In Logic Pro X, you can do this by showing the Arrangement Track (by clicking the Global Tracks button) and pressing the Add Marker button. These arrangement tracks default to 8 bars long, and can be named:

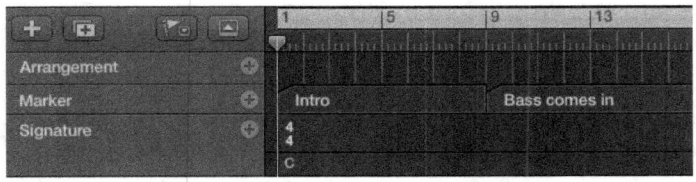

Equally, in Ableton, you can add markers in Arrangement View by right-clicking just under the playhead. You can move between these by clicking the two arrow buttons in the top-right of the Arrangement View:

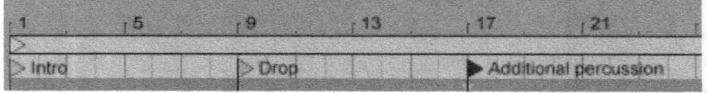

You'd be wise to add markers to mark every significant event that occurs in your composition - in electronic music this would be the introduction, first drop, first break, etc. and in rock music this would be the introduction, first verse, first chorus, etc.

Doing this will enable you to move quickly between the different areas of your track - it's easy to lose time without knowing it 'hunting' for the correct section of your track.

Use a notepad

One of the biggest challenges when reviewing your own work is to maintain a rational, objective view. It's so easy to get lost in the reviewing process. It's all too easy to make changes and then have to make further changes to adjust to your original change, or pick apart small sections without considering their impact upon your work as a whole.

I propose a simple process to review your compositions:

1. Listen to your track, writing anything wrong, along with a timestamp of when in the track the issue occurs.

2. Fix all the issues you noted. If you notice any new issues while fixing current issues, write the new issues down on a new page.

3. Once you've finished, start the process again, playing the track back and writing any issues you hear down. Either do this on a new page of paper or add to the issues you've already started on a new page.

This may seem like an arduous process, but it's actually far easier and more effective than an unstructured approach. Rather than wade through the mire of a challenging project, you can create iterations of your work. These iterations will give you an objective view of the development of your work; freeing you to make correct decisions. Your phone's notepad app will suffice if you don't have pen and paper handy:

0:30 needs more drama
0:54 start to fade hi-hats slightly
1:03 heavier sidechain required
1:30 FX wash out the mix
1:58 vox need turning down slightly
2:03 pad sound needs to be hollowed
2:35 drop is too boring
2:58 ride cymbal too tinny
3:04 more sub required
3:55 needs extra layers to feel like it's going somewhere
4:23 sound effect needs replacing with something smoother
5:03 outro needs to be more dramatic

Mix in order

A further way you can structure the editing process is to create your mixdowns in a defined order.

There are several ways to accomplish the same outcome when mixing - and this isn't always a good thing!

It helps to work in the same way each time; this consistency allows you to form mental patterns and make discoveries, improving your process.

You are welcome to adapt this as part of your workflow, because the most important element is to create a mental pattern you can vary. However, I suggest a particular order of operations when mixing:

1. Decide your initial volume levels. This allows you to establish a baseline.
2. EQ. This allows you to make any adaptions required.
3. Panning.
4. FX adjustments.
5. Levels, adjusting for what you've done in steps 2-5.

Beyond that, there are some strategies that can make the whole mixing process easier before you come to it. They are:

1. Make your effects gain-neutral. There are some effects that increase the peak volume of your track, for example, a heavy distortion. When applying these effects, try to compensate for the amplitude increase by decreasing the amplitude of the effects unit's amplitude,

monitoring your levels to get an idea of the extent of the reduction required::

2. Automating the volume of a track can often be a necessity, however unless you're working on the final mixdown these automations can work against you, forcing you to readjust the automation. If you automate the volume of a track prior to final mixdown, try automating a generic Utility function to adjust the gain of the track, keeping the mixer fader for your final mixdown.

3. Think about the secondary effects of any effects units you apply. For example, if you know you will saturate a drum track, don't EQ it until you've done so, because saturation will likely increase the amount of treble in your drum track anyway.

The final mix

Once you've finished a track, you'll likely undertake a final mixing process – to complete a final mix before you've refined your track and arrangement will only necessitate an additional final mix once you've made changes. A good final mix can take time, so having to re-do a final mix would be a wasteful use of your resources.

An even bigger waste of resources would be to send your track to be mastered, only to find that you're not happy with the master because your initial mix was wrong.

On this basis, your final mix should always be with mastering in mind. Whilst there's some variation between mastering engineers, the specifications of a correct premaster are fairly universal:

- No compression, EQ or limiting on the master output channel

- At least -7dB headroom volume, with no peaks exceeding -3dBFS

- 24-bit WAV or AIFF

- Not too hot or harsh a mix

Whilst these will become second nature to you over time, bearing these specifications in mind during your mixdown will pay huge dividends, not only in saving you time and money but in making your final product sound as brilliant as possible.

Chapter 6 – Consider Individual Tasks

When you really need to get things done, for example, if you're working to a deadline or you're creating a large batch of music, it can help to deconstruct the music-making process into small tasks to complete.

You can accomplish this through using project management software, the type that is more commonly used for software projects.

A widely used example is called Trello (available at trello.com), which allows you to create boards that track different elements of writing a track. Here is an example of a board:

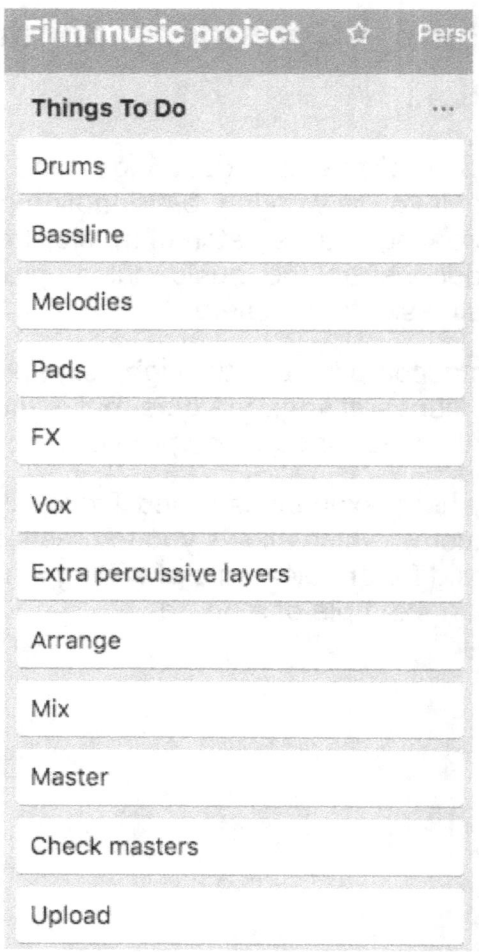

You can then add timings to give yourself hard deadlines for each element. For example, with 12 hours to complete a project, you could label them like so, with the total production time (without breaks) taking 10 hours:

Things To Do   ...

Drums - 1hr

Bassline - 30mins

Melodies - 1hr

Pads - 30mins

FX - 1hr

Vox - 1hr

Extra percussive layers - 30mins

Arrange - 1hr

Mix - 90mins

Master - 1hr

Check and amend masters - 30mins

Upload - 30mins

All you need to do then is to set a countdown timer for these individual elements and drag them into a "Done" pile once they are complete:

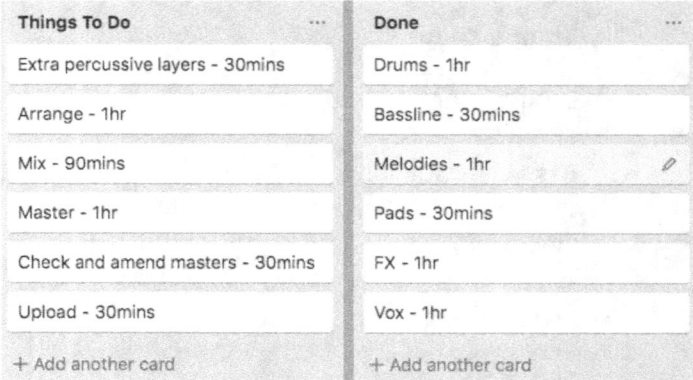

Give yourself enough timing slack in your schedule so you can take breaks and swap time between elements if required – in the example above, I may have worked on my bassline for only 20 minutes but used the extra 10 minutes to spend longer on my melodies.

Working like this, whilst not being the most friendly way of working for artistic expression, allows you to achieve strong results in very little time.

Chapter 7 – The Future

Cloud storage… Cloud mastering… AI composition…

The tips I've given you so far in this book have harnessed a mixture of discipline, organisation and technology to make you a more efficient musician.

There are always technological developments on the horizon, and many of these are designed to give you a more efficient workflow. This chapter will take you through the pros and cons of the current technological developments.

Cloud Storage

The Internet was founded upon decentralisation. Small servers scattered across the globe hosted the earliest websites. As home internet speeds increase and data storage becomes cheaper, the tech giants are placing a huge emphasis on moving our computing experience to The Cloud – whereby rather than consumers using their own computers for storage, home computers become nodes plugging into centralised data centres known as The Cloud.

This has already begun in productivity fields with Office 365 – where you can work on your Office documents at any time anywhere in the world on most contemporary computing platforms.

Google's Stadia games console also aims to break the mould, whereby your games console essentially *streams* computer games from Google's servers, meaning that Google's servers take care of all the resource-intensive graphics processing.

Splice is a company that allows you to save your DAW files to the cloud, as well as rent to own well-known plugins such as Serum and the Studio One DAW. You can also use Splice to collaborate on a fairly limited basis.

Whereas word processing documents or spreadsheets are fairly uniform, music production is made up of a huge number of unique setups – it's unlikely that any two people will have the same DAW with the same plugins and hardware instruments. This makes cloud collaboration difficult to implement for musicians.

Despite this, I venture to say that at some point in the near future, a company will have developed a fully-fledged cloud music production solution, where your DAW, samples and plugins will all be available on a platform-agnostic basis, so you will no longer have two different setups depending upon whether you're using your home studio DAW or you're on the road using your laptop. There will also be realtime collaboration possibilities, where you and a collaborator can work live on the same track. Given the challenges involved in implementing this, I'd expect the first major company to allow this will be an all-in-one solution, like Propellerhead Reason.

Until we're at that point, the cloud can be extremely helpful for storing samples in one central place – mainstream cloud storage providers like Google's Drive or Microsoft's OneDrive will even synch with your current hard drive, so that you can drag and drop samples directly from your cloud drive to your DAW.

Let's look at the advantages and disadvantages of cloud storage:

Advantages:

- Your files are available anywhere, at any time.
- Cloud storage is generally reasonably cheap.
- Data transfer speeds are usually quick if your home internet is quick.
- The search interfaces of cloud storage services are extremely fast.

Disadvantages:

- Should your internet connection fail, you cannot access your cloud files (unless you have a recent synch cached).
- Should your cloud storage provider fail, you may lose your files permanently.

- Your files are visible to the provider. There's a theoretical risk that if you upload copyrighted materials to your cloud storage provider, you may be denied access during a clampdown on copyrighted materials – and even if you can prove legal ownership of these files, the process to regain access could prove slow and arduous.

Cloud Mastering

Cloud mastering services such as LANDR or MasteringBox have grown a great deal lately. These allow you to drag-and-drop files to be immediately mastered, usually within minutes.

I find cloud mastering immensely useful for quickly mastering demos or recorded DJ mixes, as the results tend to be warm and clean.

I would not, however, recommend cloud mastering for creating final masters of tracks for releases – cloud mastering simply cannot replicate the nuanced knowledge of your genre that an experienced mastering engineer can. It also certainly can't understand the 'bigger picture' when mastering several tracks, for example understanding the dynamics of the tracks of an EP or album.

AI Composition

Taking the idea of efficient technology-aided composition to its extreme logical conclusion, a number of AI composition tools have recently appeared on the market. These tools not only help you compose your material but write the melodies themselves according to your specifications.

Prominent examples include AIVA, which was created specifically to write emotional soundtrack music. AIVA uses its internal algorithm to write, orchestrate and mix your track for you – all you have to do is download the resulting audio file. You can even pay for a commercial license which allows you to retain the copyright on AIVA-generated music.

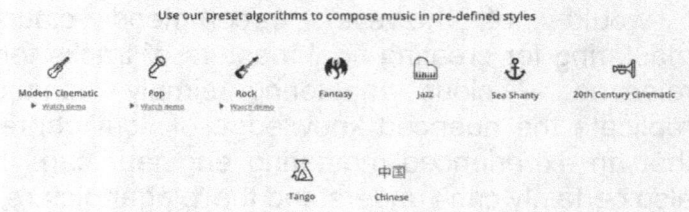

Another example is Orb Composer, which works on a standalone basis or can plug into your DAW via MIDI channels. Orb Composer initially looks like loop-based composers, the key difference being that all 'sections' within Orb Composer are in fact AI-generated melodies.

The initial internal sounds of Orb Composer on a standalone basis are unconvincing (as of writing). The melodies, however, make audial sense; you can tell that the algorithm is based upon sound research of the attributes that form good melodies. It does, however, take time and experience to create something within Orb Composer that sounds *human* – and it seems to fall short in areas that humans excel, for example tender piano melodies.

I have no doubt that given enough practice and experience working with a tool like Orb Composer, a producer could quickly create a significant portfolio of tracks using the techniques in this book combined with Orb Composer undertaking the heavy lifting of melodic composition.

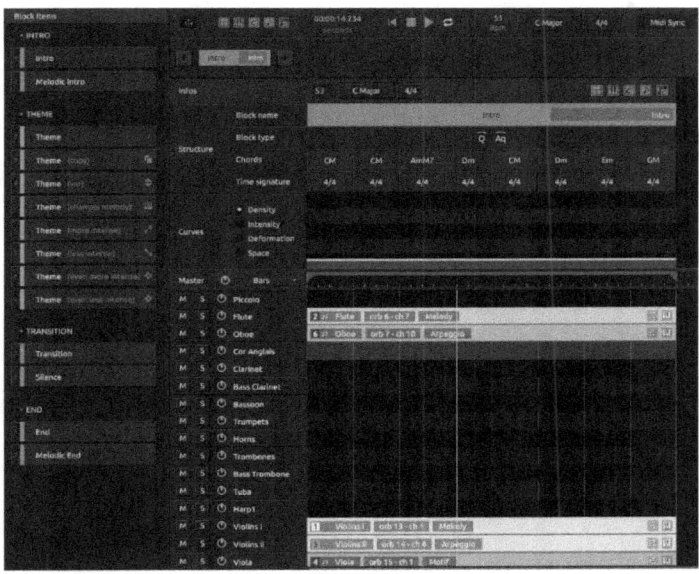

The real question, however, is what your motivation in making music is.

Are you expressing yourself through your musical creations, or are you writing music because it's your job? If it's the former, there's an unnerving feeling to divorcing yourself from the composition process. If it's the latter, there may be a happy medium where AI music generation is your partner in music composition, helping you out of creative ruts and providing you initial melodies to tweak when you happen across something interesting. It is, however, a matter of your moral perspective as an artist.

To summarise, technological development is your friend and foe – it is simply a question of what costs and risks (both financial and emotional) you're willing to take on to improve your efficiency.

Chapter 8 – Staying Creative (And What To Do When You're Not)

Fight it… Accept it…

The tips in this book will help you in terms of your creativity and productivity. But sometimes, it's easy to fall into a creative rut. This is an issue that befalls all creatives at some point, and there tends to be two main options:

1) Fight it
2) Accept it

This chapter will explain both methods.

Fight it

To fight a creative rut means to create in spite of the feeling that you lack creativity. This is the approach that many professionals take, and stems from the hypothesis that as we create, we subconsciously self-impose limitations upon our creations – and that these limitations eventually box us in, leaving us devoid of the creative spark that initially preceded them:

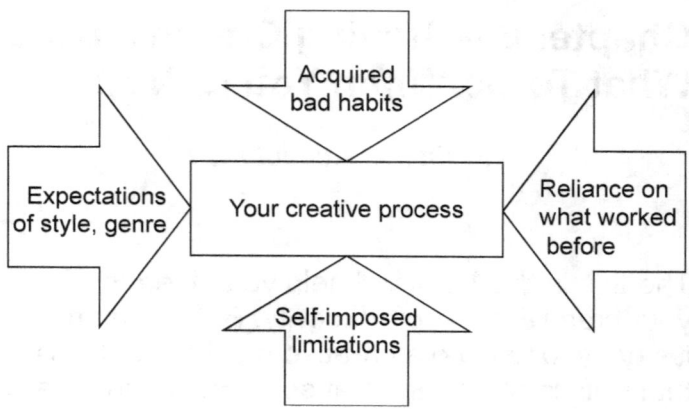

On that basis, when you get stuck in a rut, you must therefore change the parameters that limit you. Methods that will help you do this are:

Seek inspiration from other forms of art. Look at visual art, cinema, or literature – anything that gives you a feel for other people's creative processes.

2) Seek inspiration from external environments. Try going for a walk and observing your environment, or head out to a dingy underground music venue to listen to something from the cutting edge.

3) Self-impose different limitations on your work. Try writing in a different time signature, or at a different tempo, or using one instrument only.

4) Acquire a new instrument, sample or effects unit. This doesn't have to be at cost – a free VST will work. Experiment with using the presets in your work.

5) Add randomness to your work. An example is Brian Eno and Peter Schmidt's *Oblique Strategies*, which is a set of 100 cards. You pick one at random and implement the advice given. An example is "What wouldn't you do?". Another example is Roger von Oech's *A Whack on the Side of the Head* (illustrated below):

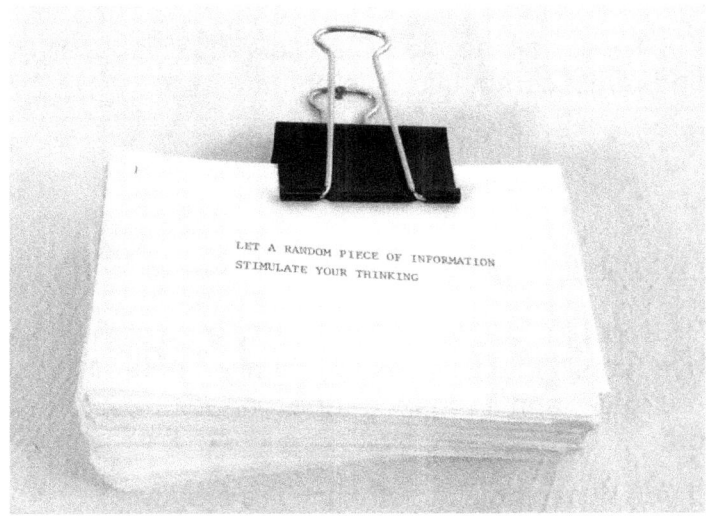

6) Create anyway. Routine can be useful when stuck in a rut, and even if you don't like the music that you create in this rut, you still gain experience. It's also possible to create brilliant work in this state, even if you don't think it's good at the time.

7) Research the latest production techniques and add these into your work.

8) Change your work destructively. Create a spare copy of the track you're stuck on and try changing instrumentations and mixes in ways that wouldn't normally make sense to you. Look for good results within your tinkering.

9) Analyze your favourite music for themes or techniques you're unfamiliar with.

10) Try to collaborate with fellow musicians, or find remix competitions to enter.

Accept it

To accept a creative rut means to accept the hypothesis that creativity is a limited natural resource, and it must be replenished once it runs out.

If you accept this hypothesis, the creative process becomes a two-part cycle:

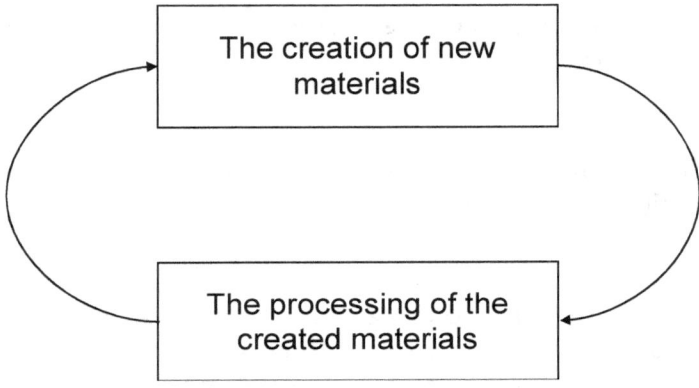

This means that when you're not actively composing music, there's a number of things you can do, for example:

1) Work on your artist profile. Is there anything you can do to better promote your work on social media, for example?

2) Send out demos/radio promos and gather feedback.

3) Create final arrangements and mixes of your music – sometimes a dispassionate ear is exactly what you need for a final version of a track.

4) Get your final mixes ready for mastering and mastered.

5) Sort your finished tracks into releases, including all metadata.

6) Are there any other avenues for releasing your music that you're yet to consider, for example self-releasing or through a production music publishing company?

7) Is music your only artistic medium? If not, work on some of your other artistic mediums. Some mediums work together well, for example your photography or visual art can be used as imagery for your releases.

8) Do you make money from your music? If so, bookkeeping and tax returns are an unfortunate fact of self-employment.

9) Explore any emerging technologies that may affect or improve your music-making process.

10) Look through your unfinished tracks for parts that you can recycle for use in future tracks.

Chapter 9 – The Whole Process

The end-to-end supply chain

I would hope that everything you've read in this book so far has made a significant impact upon your processes, however when we look at the whole process of music production, the picture looks vastly different:

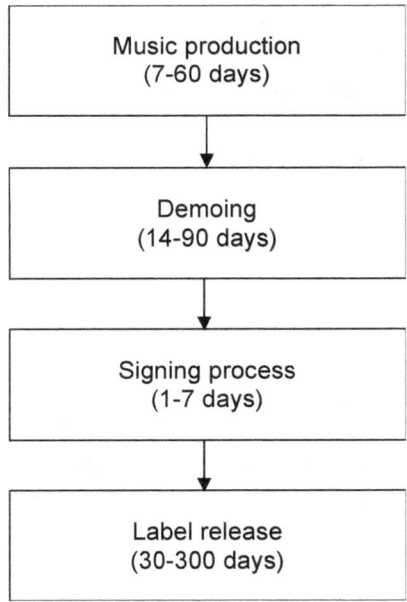

This creates an overall end-to-end time from starting the track to release of between almost two months and fifteen months – an estimation that may seem wild but is pretty realistic. This, of course, assumes that the process operates smoothly, and, for example, the label doesn't ask for revisions to the tracks or spends long periods being uncommunicative.

Even if your production process is as lean and efficient as possible, and the estimated time required for the music production element is reduced to 7-14 days, this merely brings the upper bound of the whole process down to around thirteen months.

The reason for this is that whilst your processes might be lean and efficient, your supply chain isn't – and unfortunately, it's out of your control.

There are two main approaches you can take to solve this problem – work with it, or take control.

Work with it

To take the *work with it* approach means to accept that external factors are slow and beyond your control. The only way to counteract this is to build a *pipeline*.

To build a pipeline is to accept that the timeline after you've finished your tracks is mostly out of your control, and simply to keep writing music. Once you've got enough tracks being demoed, or with labels, the delays matter less, because *something* is always happening *somewhere*.

To illustrate, imagine you have six releases, all at various stages of the pipeline:

	Status	Time in status (days)
Single 1	Released	N/A
Single 2	With label	91
Album 1	With label	35
Single 3	Signing	3
EP 1	Demo	29
EP 2	Composition	7

As you can see, if you create music regularly enough and continue to do so, your career is still relatively safe if one of your releases is delayed.

Take control

The alternative approach is to take control of the supply chain after you've written your tracks. If you're releasing digitally only, your process could be as short as this:

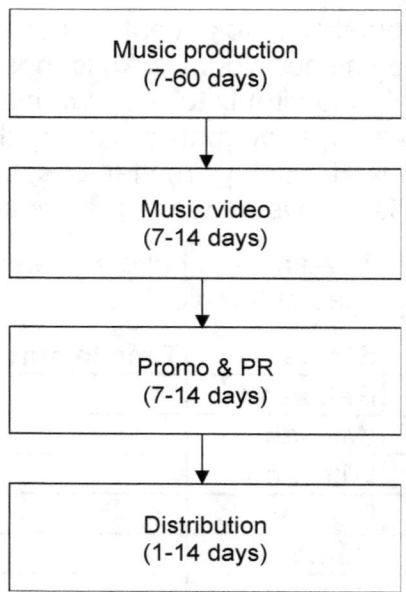

Physical distribution is more complex, for example if you're releasing on vinyl:

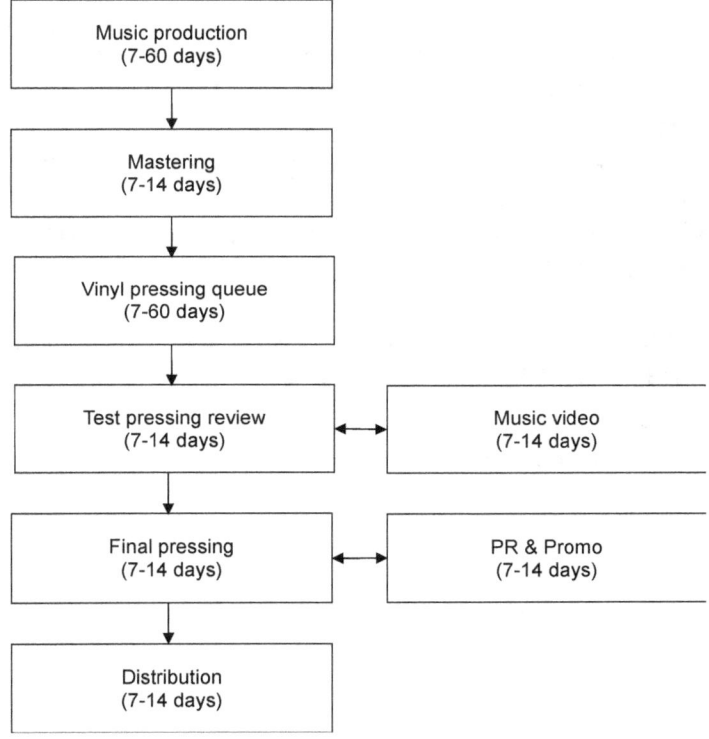

Even if you work on the video and promo simultaneously with the pressing, this timeline can take anything between 35 days and six months.

However, that's not to say that you can't find efficiencies. Within each of these nodes, you can find efficiencies within their processes. For example, assume the above timeline is for a London-based artist working with their favoured Berlin-based pressing plant. The artist could do the following:

1) Limit their production time to 30 days
2) Pre-book their slot with the mastering engineer
3) Call around to find pressing plants in the local area with spare capacity
4) Physically go to the pressing plant to pick up the test pressings

After making these efficiency savings, the timeline would look like this:

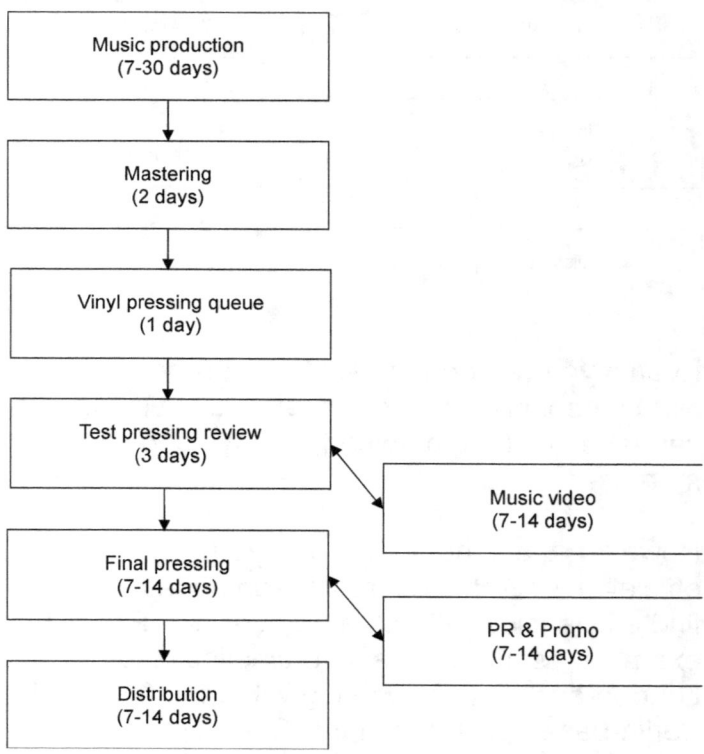

The release would now take between 27 days and just over two months – cutting time from the initial production to the final release to a third of its original upper bound.

That's not to say, however, that there are no downsides to the *work with it* approach.

To self-release your music, you'll essentially be starting your own label. This means you'll be doing the promo, video and social media yourself. This is time that you won't be spending writing music, and so it will have a big effect on the amount of music you put out there.

Alternatively, you could outsource these elements to external companies, and theoretically have the best of both worlds, but this will cost money, and unless you're in the top 1% of producers your release probably won't make much.

On top of that, there will be an initial investment in starting your own label – setting up social media profiles and gaining traction, setting up with a distributor, setting up a company and separate bank account (if you're that way inclined) and compiling mailing lists of possible fans and reviewers. This, of course, is also time spent not making music.

Which approach you pick is a matter of compromise and personal preference. There are no right answers – the only solace is that this kind of headache is one that any company or person that's ever made anything has had to go through!

Chapter 9 – Efficiency Analysis

So far in this book I've covered some tips for making your music production process more efficient. These tips will help you hugely over the long term, but the real joy comes from creating your own efficiencies. This chapter will teach you how to do exactly that.

The first element of doing this is to capture data. You can do this by screen recording a production session. It sounds bizarre, and it sounds like a waste of time, but holding up a mirror to yourself is always useful - think of how you don't hear mistakes in your music until you play it to someone else.

Time cost calculations

It's easy to make time savings when you look at the long term.

For example, let's say you only produce on the weekends, averaging 6 hours per weekend. That's 312 hours per year - let's round that down to 300.

Let's say there's a process you do five times per hour, and the process takes one minute. Halving the time it would take to undertake that process would give you back two-and-a-half minutes per hour - or twelve and a half hours of production time across the year. That means that if you spend less than twelve and a half hours on the act of improving that process, you've made a profit over the coming year.

Marginal gains translate to huge gains across a long enough timeline.

The equation to understand time saved over a year is simple. Please don't be intimidated by the maths here – try to complete these calculations on a piece of paper with a calculator if you're struggling with the mental arithmetic.

First, you need to estimate how many hours per year you spend producing music. You can do this by estimating the number of hours you spend producing per week and multiplying this by 52:

$$A*52$$

Where a = number of hours you spend producing music per week.

Once you have this number, write it down and call it y.

Then, look at how much time you spend doing a particular task per year. To accomplish this, you need to find the average handling time of the task. Find five instances of you undertaking the task, and measure (with a stopwatch) how much time (in seconds) each instance of the task took. Add up the seconds and divide the total number by five to understand the Average Handling Time of the task.

Then, estimate the number of times you undertake that task per hour.

Once you have that number, you can calculate how much time you spend undertaking the task across the year:

$$AHT*f$$

Where f is the frequency of the task per hour. Use a decimal, e.g. 0.25 if you undertake the task once every four hours.

Once you have that figure, call it x.

Then, all you need to do is multiply by the Y figure you wrote earlier (which is the number of hours you spend producing music over the course of the year), and you understand the impact that the task has on your production time over the course of a year.

Here's the formula in a format you can return to:

$$(a*52)*(AHT*f)$$

If you struggle with maths, that's ok. This is a numerical method of proving the fact that by spending time making a process more efficient now, you save yourself huge amounts of time in the future. It's that simple.

You can use the technique in this chapter to create your own efficiencies in music production – efficiencies I haven't spotted. Watch a recording of you producing music and think to yourself:

- Is this a task I undertake regularly?
- Is there a better way of accomplishing it?
- Does it take up time I could spend doing a more creative activity?

If something ticks these boxes, make it more efficient! You won't regret it. The fewer snags and drags you have holding you back from making good music, the happier and better you'll be as a producer. You can use the mathematical process in this chapter to calculate the gains of making other efficiencies in your life. You could even use it to work out whether or not the purchase of a dishwasher would be justified!

Process analysis

Beyond the mathematics of calculating *what* efficiencies you would gain from making a process more efficient, there's the matter of *how*.

Most of the tips in this book are a result of this type of analysis, and already form a comprehensive suite of ways to make your music production more efficient. However, they also assume that there aren't additional processes that you spend your time doing. For these processes, this section will teach you the method to make these more efficient.

The first step is to map out the individual steps of the whole process. You can do this using pen and paper, post-it notes or software like Microsoft Visio or www.draw.io. Complex processes can take a long time to map out – I've seen business processes cover an entire office wall when drawn on post-it notes! However, smaller music production processes will be far leaner.

As an example, let's say you are a digital label owner paying your artists their royalties. This is an example of what that process will look like:

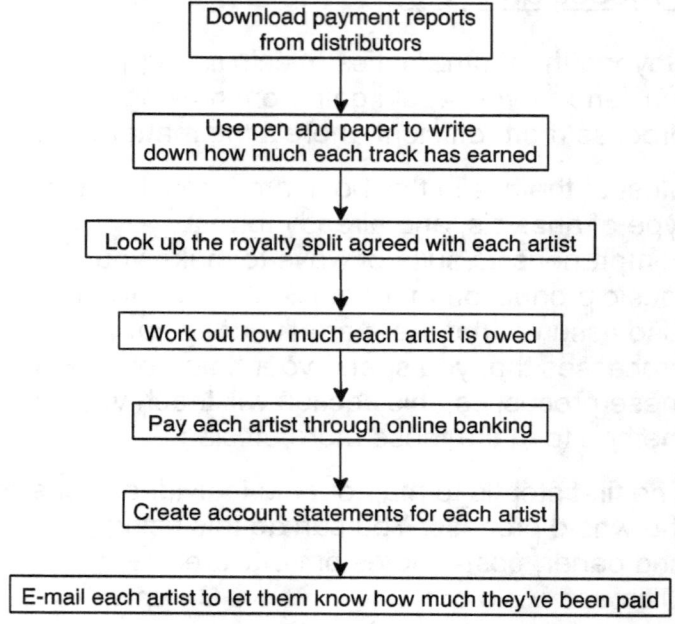

I appreciate that the actual process will undoubtedly be more complex than this, but let's use it as an example without getting bogged down too much in detail.

Once you've mapped each step in the process, it's time to look at each step. With each step, there are three options to find efficiencies. In order of preference, these are:

1) Eliminate

2) Automate

3) Replace

4) Delegate

Let's look at each step through the lens of the first – is there anything you can eliminate?

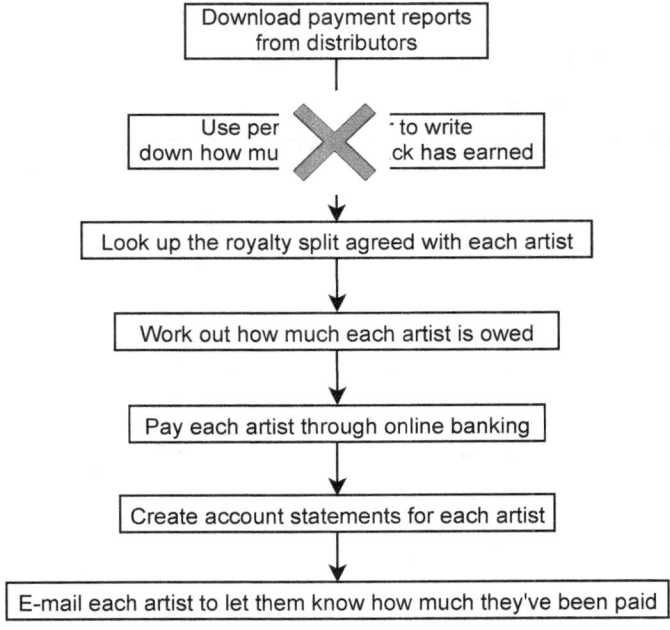

We can get rid of the pen and paper step; we already have the earnings on the spreadsheet file we've downloaded.

Next, is there anything we can automate?

Admittedly, I'm a spreadsheet nerd, so in my case, looking up the royalty split and working out how much each artist is owed can be automated using LOOKUP and standard calculation formulas.

Beyond that, most banks now support digital bulk payments – so you can load your payments into your bank and have the payouts occur automatically. With some nifty macro programming work, you can even ask your spreadsheet to automatically output a bulk payment schedule for your bank.

Now that's done, you can safely say you've automated three steps of your process:

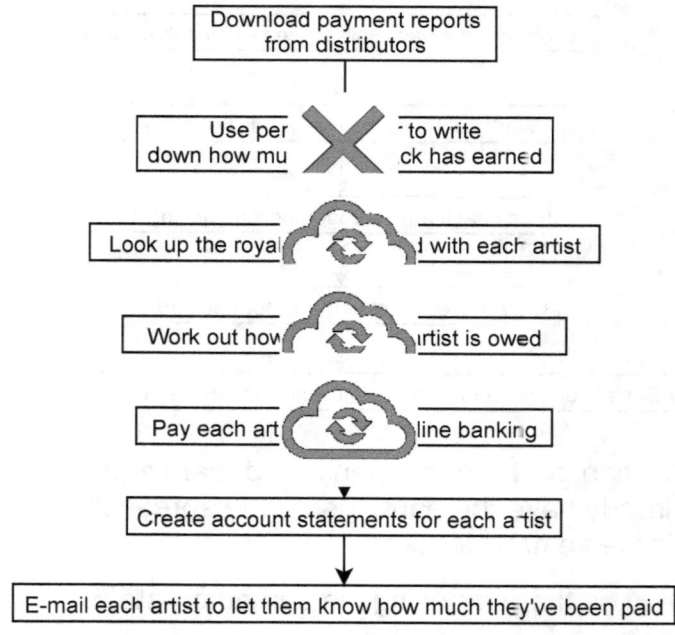

Now let's look at a possible replacement – you currently create account statements for each artist. But is that truly necessary? Unless you're contractually obliged to create a statement in a particular format, it would be far easier to create a simple sheet and send your artist a cloud link, rather than the hassle of attaching a statement – as not all your artists will bother to read a statement.

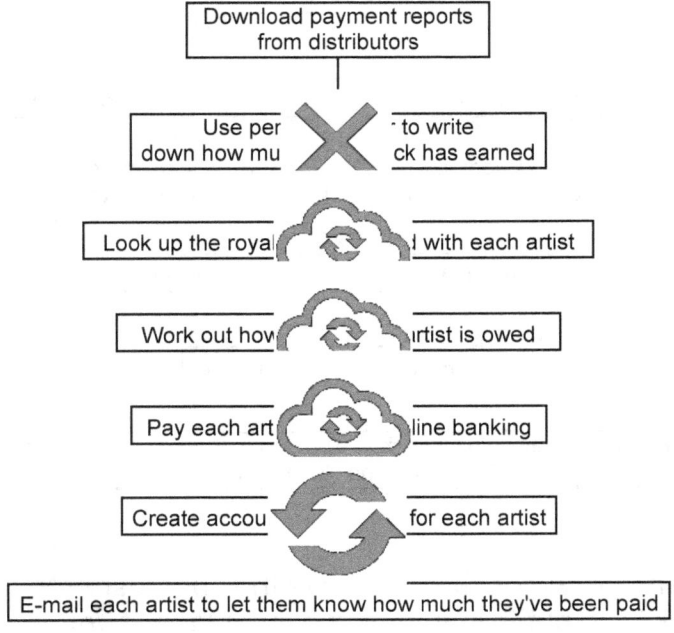

You may have also spotted that it's easy enough to automate e-mails. I've chosen not to automate this step, as a personal e-mail to each artist may do much to maintain a personal relationship with each artist – remember, efficiency is always a choice!

Given the elimination and automation we've put in place, the new process looks like this:

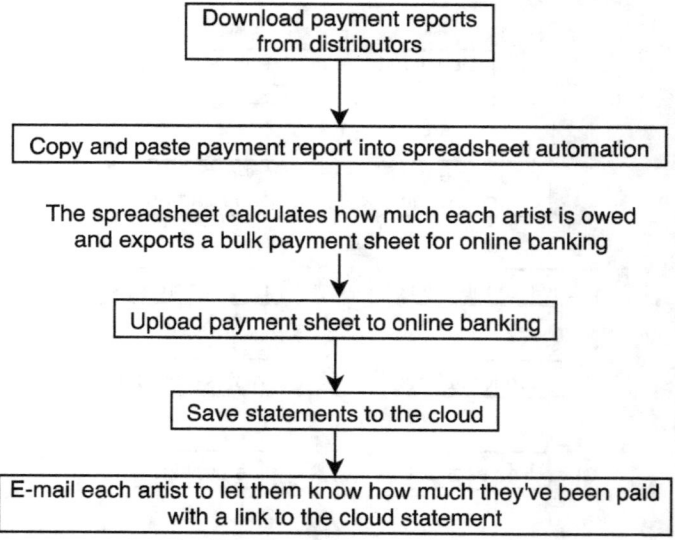

This assumes that you have the spreadsheet skills to put this automation into place. If you don't, look at option 4 – delegation. You could either pay someone to make your royalty payments for you, or you could ask a geeky friend, or failing that pay someone, to create the solution for you.

I know that this process analysis has felt specific, and new, but process analysis is a wonderful tool that can help you not only in music production, but in every facet of your life.

The process is circular – if you apply process analysis to other parts of your life that take up your time, this gives you more time for your (efficient) music production!

Conclusion

To conclude, once you've implemented the ideas in this book, reward yourself! You will find that your music production sessions become more fun, more spontaneous and more creative because you implemented the ideas in this book.

Spend the time you save however you like, whether that's going for a walk, spending more time with your friends and family, or improving your music production skills.

I hope, now you've internalised the thinking behind creating efficiencies, that you understand that being efficient is not a cold, dispassionate, artificial way of thinking, but a liberating one.

You write music because you love music.

Efficiency simply removes the barriers between you and working on what you love.

Thank you for reading this book.

Keyboard shortcuts

(Near) Universal DAW keyboard shortcuts

Function	Shortcut
New file	⌘/Ctrl + N
Select All	⌘/Ctrl + A
Copy	⌘/Ctrl + C
Cut	⌘/Ctrl + X
Paste	⌘/Ctrl + V
Undo	⌘/Ctrl + Z
Save	⌘/Ctrl + S
Save As	⌘/Ctrl + Shift + S
Open	⌘/Ctrl + O
Play/Pause	Space
Toggle automation mode	A
Quit	⌘/Ctrl + Q
Enter a manual value (e.g. mixer level)	Click/double-click
Type in value	Number keys
Confirm value	Enter/Return
Abort entering value	Esc
Solo multiple tracks	⌘/Ctrl + click

Further reading

<u>Further reading on the assembly line and lean manufacturing</u>

1) Wee, H. and Wu, S. (2009). *Lean supply chain and its effect on product cost and quality: a case study on Ford Motor Company.* [online] Available at:
https://www.researchgate.net/profile/Simon_Wu3/publication/235250372_Lean_Supply_Chain_and_Its_Effect_on_Product_Cost_and_Quality-A_Case_Study_on_Ford_Motor_Company/links/59489c37458515db1fd7104c/Lean-Supply-Chain-and-Its-Effect-on-Product-Cost-and-Quality-A-Case-Study-on-Ford-Motor-Company.pdf

2) Artoflean.com. (2019). *Toyota Production System Basic Handbook.* [online] Available at: http://artoflean.com/wp-content/uploads/2019/01/Basic_TPS_Handbook.pdf

3) Ericsson, K., Krampe, R. and Tesch-Römer, C. (1993). The role of deliberate practice in the acquisition of expert performance. *Psychological Review*, [online] 100(3), pp.363-406. Available at:
http://projects.ict.usc.edu/itw/gel/EricssonDeliberatePracticePR93.pdf.

Further reading on 10,000 hours

1) Ericsson, K., Krampe, R. and Tesch-Römer, C. (1993). The role of deliberate practice in the acquisition of expert performance. *Psychological Review*, [online] 100(3), pp.363-406. Available at: http://projects.ict.usc.edu/itw/gel/EricssonDeliberatePracticePR93.pdf.

2) Gladwell, M. (2009). *Outliers*. Penguin.

Further reading on flow

Nakamura, J.; Csikszentmihályi, M. (20 December 2001). "Flow Theory and Research". In C. R. Snyder Erik Wright, and Shane J. Lopez. Handbook of Positive Psychology. Oxford University Press. pp. 195–206. ISBN 978-0-19-803094-2.

Pitchfork.com. (2019). In the Flow: A Musician's Guide to a Creative Mind State | Pitchfork. [online] Available at: https://pitchfork.com/features/sponsor-content/in-the-flow/.

Sawyer, R. (2006). Group creativity: musical performance and collaboration. Psychology of Music, 34(2), pp.148-165.

Vass, M., Carroll, J. and Shaffer, C. (2019). Supporting Creativity in Problem Solving

Environments. Proceedings of the Fourth Creativity and Cognition Conference, [online] pp.31-37. Available at: http://jigcell.cs.vt.edu/Pubs/Creativity.pdf

www.ingramcontent.com/pod-product-compliance
Lightning Source LLC
Chambersburg PA
CBHW071905070526
44583CB00016B/1851